I0479740

Profit Oriented Manual For Businesses

"Tips for Creating a Profitable and Sustainable Company"

Michael D. Shearer

Copyright

Table of content

Introduction

Welcome to the world of profits! This book is the definitive guide to gaining success in the business world by concentrating on the bottom line. Whether you are a seasoned entrepreneur or just starting, this book will give you the skills and methods you need to boost revenues and develop a sustainable firm.

In the pages ahead, Welcome to the world of profits! This book is the definitive guide to gaining success in the business world by concentrating on the bottom line. Whether you are a seasoned entrepreneur or just starting, this book will give you the skills and methods you need to boost revenues and develop a sustainable firm.

In the pages ahead, you will uncover the secrets of great firms that have consistently provided excellent profits year after year. You will learn how to discover and capitalize on profitable possibilities, how to organize your processes for optimal efficiency, and how to establish a winning team that is focused on generating growth and profitability.

Yet this book is not simply about generating money. It is also about generating value for your consumers, developing enduring connections with your stakeholders, and having a good effect on the world around you. By taking a profit-oriented attitude to the company, you will not only achieve financial success but also establish a legacy that will last for generations.

Hence, if you are ready to take your company to the next level, this book is for you. Let's dig in and discover the potential of earnings!

The Significance of Profitability in Business

Profitability is the cornerstone of the success of every firm. It is a crucial indicator that reveals if a corporation is producing enough money to cover its expenditures and produce a profit. A productive firm can maintain itself over the long term, invest in growth possibilities, and create returns for its stockholders.

There are various reasons why profitability is crucial in business:

1. **Financial stability:** A prosperous firm is financially secure and can weather economic downturns, changes in the market, or unanticipated costs. A firm that continuously earns profits may build up financial reserves, pay off debt, and reinvest in the company's future.

2. **Growth possibilities:** Successful firms have the flexibility to invest in growth opportunities, such as extending their product lines, entering new markets, or purchasing other companies. These investments might allow the firm to enhance its income and earnings in the long run.

3. **Attract investors:** Investors are more inclined to invest in a productive firm because they can see a clear return on their investment. Profitability also suggests that the firm is well-managed and has a solid financial basis.

4. **Competitive advantage:** Profitability may provide a corporation with a competitive edge in the market. A thriving firm may spend on marketing and advertising, research and development, and staff training, which can allow it to distinguish itself from rivals and attract more clients.

5. **Employee satisfaction:** Successful organizations may afford to give greater remuneration and benefits packages to their workers. This may boost employee happiness and retention, which in turn can lead to higher productivity and profitability.

In summary, profitability is important to the success of every firm. It offers financial stability, and growth prospects attract investors, gives a competitive edge and enhances employee happiness. Companies should concentrate on producing revenues and minimizing expenditures to guarantee their long-term survival and success.

What it means to be Profit Oriented

Being profit-oriented indicates that a firm is mainly focused on making profits and expanding its bottom line. A profit-oriented firm strives to increase its income while limiting its expenditures to obtain the maximum potential profit margin.

Being profit-oriented is not always a bad characteristic. Profitability is vital for the long-term success of any firm. Yet, a corporation that is primarily focused on profits may compromise other key components of the business, such as customer happiness, employee contentment, and social responsibility.

The following are some characteristics of a profit-oriented business:

1. **Revenue-driven:** A profit-oriented firm is largely focused on raising its revenue. It may emphasize sales above other parts of the firm, such as customer happiness or product quality.

2. **Cost-conscious:** A profit-oriented firm is focused on decreasing its expenditures to maximize its profit margin. It may be prepared to cut shortcuts or decrease expenses in areas like employee perks, marketing, or product development.

3. **Short-term focus:** A profit-oriented firm is focused on reaching short-term financial objectives, such as fulfilling quarterly sales targets or growing profit margins. It may be less concerned with long-term sustainability or developing a great brand image.

4. **Competitive mindset:** A profit-oriented firm may be very competitive and focused on exceeding its competitors. It may emphasize obtaining market share above creating good connections with consumers or suppliers.

Although being profit-oriented might be advantageous in certain situations, it is necessary for organizations to also consider other variables such as customer pleasure, employee contentment, and social responsibility. A firm that is primarily focused on earnings may compromise these key components of the business, which may lead to long-term troubles.

In conclusion, being profit-oriented indicates that a firm is mainly focused on making profits and boosting its bottom line. Although profitability is vital, it is equally necessary for organizations to examine other variables that contribute to long-term success and sustainability.

PART I

Creating a Basis for Profitability

Creating a Basis for Profitability

Establishing a foundation for profitability is crucial for the long-term success of any organization. A thriving firm needs a solid foundation that includes a clear vision, a strong business strategy, excellent financial management, and a focus on giving value to consumers.

These are some critical measures for developing a foundation for profitability:

1. **Create a clear vision**: A clear vision helps to generate a feeling of purpose for the firm and gives a path for attaining long-term success. The vision should be conveyed clearly to all stakeholders, including workers, consumers, and investors.

2. **Develop a good business plan:** A great business plan spells forth the strategies and tactics required to attain the goal. The

strategy should contain a complete study of the market, competitors, target customers, and financial predictions.

3. **Concentrate on offering value to customers:** Consumers are the heartbeat of every company, and delivering value to them is vital for developing a prosperous firm. This includes knowing their requirements, preferences, and pain areas and producing goods or services that satisfy those demands.

4. **Adopt good financial management:** Successful financial management comprises controlling expenditures, optimizing income, and ensuring that the firm adequate cash flow to satisfy its responsibilities. This involves defining clear financial objectives, monitoring important financial measures, and periodically analyzing financial performance.

5. **Invest in the proper people and resources:** A prosperous firm needs a strong team of workers who are talented,

motivated, and aligned with the business goal. This involves investing in staff training, growth, and retention, as well as the necessary tools and resources required to support their job.

6. Constantly monitor and modify: Establishing a thriving company demands a commitment to continually evaluate and alter plans and tactics depending on market input and changing conditions. This entails frequently assessing performance data, collecting input from customers and staff, and making improvements as appropriate.

7. Establish realistic financial objectives: Companies should create realistic financial goals that are linked with their entire strategy. Objectives should be explicit, quantifiable, and time-bound and should include revenue goals, cost targets, and profit margins.

8. **Managing expenditures:** Controlling expenses are crucial to profitability. Companies should check their spending constantly, search for possibilities to minimize costs, and prevent wasteful expenditures.

9. **Understand your market:** Companies should have a strong awareness of their market, including consumer wants and preferences, competitive environment, and industry trends. This information may help organizations discover growth prospects, establish successful marketing strategies, and distinguish themselves from the competition.

10. **Build a strong value proposal:** A good value proposition is vital for acquiring and maintaining clients. Companies should convey their unique value proposition, highlight the advantages of their goods or services, and underline how they address client issues.

11. **Invest in technology:** Investment in technology may help firms simplify processes, boost efficiency, and cut expenses. This might involve installing software for accounting and financial management, customer relationship management, and inventory management.

12. **Monitor financial performance:** Companies should frequently assess their financial performance to ensure that they are on track to fulfill their objectives. This involves monitoring revenue, costs, profit margins, and cash flow, and making changes as appropriate.

In conclusion, developing a foundation for success involves a clear vision, a good business strategy, efficient financial management, a focus on offering value to consumers, investing in the appropriate people and resources, and a willingness to regularly review and adapt strategies and tactics. By following these principles, firms may develop a strong basis for long-term prosperity and success.

Chapter 1

Understanding Your Business Model

Knowing your company model is a vital step in developing a lucrative firm. A business model is a framework that defines how your firm develops, delivers, and collects value. It explains your target clients, the items or services you provide, how you create money, and how you manage expenses. By knowing your company model, you may identify possible obstacles and opportunities, make strategic choices, and optimize profitability.

These are some crucial factors to consider while analyzing your company model:

1. **Client segments:** Determine your target customers and their demands. This will enable you to personalize your items or services to fit their expectations and preferences.

2. **Value proposition:** Describe the distinctive value you give to your consumers that sets you apart from your competition. This might be your quality, pricing, convenience, or customer service.

3. **Revenue streams:** Identify how you make income from your goods or services. This might be via sales, subscriptions, advertising, or other sources.

4. **Channels:** Determine the routes through which you reach your clients, such as via internet sales, brick-and-mortar shops, or social media.

5. **Core activities:** Identify the primary activities necessary to supply your goods or

services, such as manufacturing, marketing, or customer support.

6. **Important resources:** Determine the resources necessary to support your core tasks, such as employees, equipment, or technology.

7. **Partnerships:** Identify any partnerships or collaborations that are essential to supply your goods or services, such as suppliers or distributors.

8. **Cost structure:** Understand your cost structure, including fixed and variable expenditures, to guarantee that your organization is viable.

By knowing your business model, you can make strategic choices that will help you develop your firm and boost profitability. You may find places where you can decrease expenses, enhance your pricing approach, or grow your consumer base. It may also help you remain competitive and respond to changes in the industry.

In conclusion, knowing your business strategy is crucial for developing a prosperous firm. It helps you discover your target consumers, unique value proposition, income streams, channels, key activities, critical resources, collaborations, and cost structure. By maximizing these factors, you may increase profitability and assure the long-term success of your firm.

The Importance of Business Models in Profitability

Business models are vital in assessing the profitability of a corporation. A business model is a framework that defines how a firm develops, delivers, and collects value. It is the plan that defines how a firm produces income and controls expenses to attain profitability.

These are some ways that company models might affect profitability:

1. **Revenue streams:** A business model identifies the numerous ways a corporation might earn money. For example, a firm may create money via the sale of items, services, or subscriptions. The price strategy, the target market, and the distribution channels are all aspects that might affect revenue streams. A well-designed business model may help a firm optimize its income sources and achieve profitability.

2. **Cost structure:** A business model also impacts the cost structure of a corporation. This covers the cost of manufacturing products or services, overhead expenditures, and running expenses. By optimizing the cost structure, a corporation may cut expenses and boost profitability. For example, a firm that depends on a subscription-based business model may have reduced

manufacturing costs but greater marketing expenditures to attract new customers.

3. **Competitive advantage:** A well-designed business model may provide a corporation with a competitive edge. By distinguishing its goods or services, a firm may attract more consumers and generate income. For example, a firm that provides a unique product or service may be able to demand a premium price, which may improve revenue and profitability.

4. **Flexibility:** A business model that is flexible and adaptable may assist a firm to adjust to changes in the market and preserve profitability. For example, a corporation that has numerous income sources may be able to modify its strategy if one revenue stream becomes less lucrative.

5. **Scalability:** A scalable business plan may assist a firm to raise its income without a commensurate rise in expenses. This may

boost profitability by enhancing the efficiency of the firm. For example, a software firm that sells its product via a subscription-based model may be able to expand its income without a major rise in production expenses.

In conclusion, business models play a significant part in determining the success of a firm. A well-designed business model may maximize income streams, minimize expenses, offer a competitive edge, provide flexibility, and boost scalability. By concentrating on the creation and execution of an effective business model, a firm may enhance its profitability and achieve long-term success.

How to Assess and Enhance Your Business Model

A business model is the cornerstone of every successful firm. It highlights the company's value offer, revenue streams, target customers, and important resources. Nonetheless, a business model must be continuously examined and changed to guarantee its relevance in the ever-changing business environment.

These are some measures you may take to examine and enhance your company model:

1. **Evaluate your present business model:** Begin by assessing your current business model to find its strengths and limitations. This might involve a SWOT analysis to discover areas where you shine and areas that need development.

2. **Evaluate market trends and consumer needs:** Keep up to speed with industry changes and consumer preferences to ensure that your company strategy is

aligned with their evolving demands. Evaluate client comments, reviews, and complaints to uncover areas where you may enhance your product.

3. **Identify opportunities for improvement:** Utilize the information acquired from your evaluation to find areas for improvement. This might involve adjusting your price approach, extending your product range, or boosting your customer service.

4. **Create a new business model:** Based on the areas for improvement identified, build a new business model that tackles these difficulties. This may include shifting your income streams, target customers, or important resources.

5. **Test your new business model:** Execute your new business model on a modest scale to assess its efficacy. This might entail completing market research, pilot

testing, or introducing a restricted version of your product or service.

6. **Measure the results:** After you have deployed your new business model, assess its success. This might involve measuring revenue, customer happiness, and other related variables. Utilize this knowledge to create additional changes to your company model.

7. **Iterate and refine:** Utilize the input gained from testing and measurement to make additional adjustments to your business model. This is a continuing process that demands continuous development to remain ahead of the competition and fulfill the increasing requirements of your consumers.

In essence, assessing and enhancing your business model is crucial to the success of your firm. It takes a comprehensive examination of your present model, analyzing market trends and consumer demands, finding areas for improvement, building a new model, testing, measuring, and iterating. By consistently improving your business model, you may remain ahead of the competition and maintain the long-term survival of your firm.

Chapter 2

Finding Your Key Metrics

Finding critical metrics is a crucial aspect of operating a successful company. Metrics, or key performance indicators (KPIs), are used to monitor the success of your organization and suggest areas for development. With a profit-oriented book, there are numerous crucial measures that you should concentrate on to guarantee that your book is producing revenue and profitability.

• **Sales:** The most apparent statistic for a profit-oriented book is sales. You should monitor the number of books sold, the money produced, and the average price per book. This can assist you to discover which marketing and sales methods are working, and which are not.

• **Customer acquisition cost (CAC):** CAC quantifies the cost of obtaining a new client. This covers marketing and advertising charges, as well as any other costs related to obtaining new consumers. To optimize profitability, you should attempt to maintain your CAC as low as feasible.

• **Conversion rate:** Conversion rate indicates the proportion of website visitors who buy your book. This number is crucial since it enables you to find places where you can enhance your website, sales copy, or other marketing efforts to boost conversions.

• **Customer lifetime value (CLTV):** CLTV represents the total amount of income that a customer will create during their lifetime as a client. This indicator is crucial since it enables you to determine the long-term profitability of your book.

- **Return on investment (ROI):** ROI quantifies the amount of income earned relative to the amount of money spent on marketing and other costs. A high ROI shows that your marketing activities are productive and create a favorable return.

- **Reviews and ratings:** Reviews and ratings are significant since they may affect sales and consumer impressions of your book. You should watch the number of reviews, the average rating, and the mood of the reviews to find areas where you can enhance the book and its promotion.

- **Profit margin:** Profit margin quantifies the amount of profit earned for each book sold. This statistic is significant because it enables you to determine how much profit you are earning on each sale and may assist you to find areas where you can cut expenditures or boost income.

In conclusion, selecting essential indicators for your profit-oriented book is vital to determining the health of your company and making educated choices regarding marketing and other costs. By watching these KPIs, you may find areas for improvement and adjust your marketing and sales strategy to maximize revenue.

The Significance of Measurements in Monitoring Profitability

Metrics are vital in measuring profitability in a profit-oriented book since they assist organizations to assess how well they are doing financially. These measurements give vital insights into the business's revenue, costs, and profit margins, which may be utilized to make educated choices regarding the company's future development and performance.

These are some reasons why metrics are vital in measuring success in a profit-oriented book:

• **Measure financial performance:** Metrics give a tool to measure the financial performance of an organization. By measuring variables like as sales, costs, and profit margins, companies may acquire a better knowledge of their financial health and make educated choices about how to enhance their profitability.

• **Find opportunities for improvement:** Metrics may assist firms to discover areas where they can increase their profitability. For example, if a firm is spending too much money on marketing and not receiving a return on investment, it might modify its approach to enhance its profitability.

• **Establish objectives and targets:** Metrics may be utilized to define specific goals and targets for the firm to attain. For example, a firm may establish a target to raise its profit margins by a given percentage during the following year. Metrics may be used to measure progress towards these targets and alter methods as required.

- **Make data-driven choices:** Metrics equip organizations with data to make educated decisions about the company's financial destiny. For example, if a corporation is contemplating expanding into a new market, it may utilize metrics to analyze the potential profitability of that market and make an educated choice.

- **Enhance communication:** Metrics may increase communication inside a firm by offering common knowledge of financial performance. When everyone in the firm is monitoring the same metrics, it may assist to align goals and ensure everyone is working towards the same objectives.

In conclusion, metrics are crucial in measuring profitability in a profit-oriented book. They give firms a tool to monitor financial performance, identify areas for development, define objectives and targets, make data-driven choices, and enhance communication. By measuring indicators, firms may increase their profitability and assure their long-term success.

How to Identify and Monitor Your Key Metrics

If you're operating a company, monitoring your key metrics is vital for gauging your performance and discovering areas where you can improve. Here are some actions you may take to identify and monitor your critical metrics:

1. **Establish your company objectives:** Before you can determine your important

KPIs, you need to describe your business goals. These objectives should be explicit, quantifiable, and reachable. For example, your aim can be to raise sales by 10% in the following quarter.

2. **Define your key metrics:** After you have identified your company objectives, you can determine the essential metrics that will help you assess progress toward those goals. These measurements should be directly tied to your objectives and should be measurable. For example, if you aim to raise revenue, your important indicators may include total revenue, average revenue per client, and customer acquisition cost.

3. **Establish objectives for your key metrics:** After you have identified your important metrics, you need to set targets for each of them. These aims should be explicit and reasonable and should be based on previous data or industry standards. For example, if your current client acquisition

cost is $50, you may set a goal to lower it to $40.

4. **Monitor your key metrics:** After you have selected your key metrics and established objectives, you need to track them consistently to assess your progress toward your goals. You may monitor your metrics using a spreadsheet or specialized software, and you should update your measurements periodically, such as weekly or monthly.

5. **Assess your metrics:** Monitoring your metrics is only effective if you utilize the data to make educated choices. You should review your analytics periodically to detect trends and patterns, and to identify areas where you can improve. For example, if you discover that your client acquisition cost is growing, you may evaluate if there are chances to optimize your marketing or sales procedures.

6. **Take action based on your metrics:** Lastly, you need to take action based on the

insights you acquire from recording and analyzing your data. If you discover areas where you can improve, you need to build a strategy to target those areas and monitor your progress toward improving your metrics.

In short, selecting and monitoring your key metrics is critical for gauging your performance and discovering areas where you may enhance your profitability. By establishing your objectives, identifying your key metrics, setting targets, monitoring your metrics, evaluating your data, and taking action based on your insights, you can guarantee that your firm is on the route to success.

Chapter 3

Creating a Financial Plan

Creating a financial strategy is vital for every profit-oriented firm to guarantee its long-term survival and profitability. A financial plan is a thorough roadmap that includes the company's financial objectives, strategies, and action actions to attain those goals.

These are some critical measures to establish a financial strategy for a profit-oriented business:

Establish Financial Goals: The first stage in building a financial strategy is to identify the company's financial objectives. These objectives should be explicit, quantifiable, reachable, relevant, and time-bound. Some examples of financial objectives include growing revenue, lowering expenditures, enhancing profitability, and expanding market share.

Examine Financial Statements: The next stage is to study the company's financial statements, including the balance sheet, income statement, and cash flow statement. This research will give insights into the company's financial health, profitability, liquidity, and solvency.

Build a Budget: Based on the financial objectives and analysis of the financial accounts, develop a budget for the following year. The budget should contain predicted income, spending, and cash flow, along with assumptions and contingencies. The budget should be reviewed often to ensure that the organization continues on track.

Create Strategies: Based on the financial objectives and budget, establish methods to attain those goals. For example, if the aim is to grow income, the strategy may involve releasing new items, expanding into new areas, or boosting marketing and advertising activities. If the aim is to cut expenditures, the technique may involve simplifying operations, renegotiating contracts, or eliminating employees.

Monitor Performance: After the financial strategy is in place, it's necessary to review the company's performance periodically. This will assist you to detect any deviations from the plan and make appropriate revisions. Frequent monitoring will also assist to guarantee that the firm continues on pace to meet its financial objectives.

Evaluate and Adjust: Lastly, assess the financial plan frequently and make required modifications depending on changing conditions, such as changes in the market, competition, or regulatory environment. A financial plan is not a static document, and it should be revised periodically to reflect the current realities of the corporate environment.

In conclusion, having a financial strategy is vital for a profit-oriented firm to meet its financial objectives, secure its long-term viability, and remain ahead of the competition. By identifying financial objectives, examining financial statements, making a budget, devising strategies, monitoring performance, and reviewing and revising constantly, organizations may achieve financial success and development.

Developing Realistic Income and Expenditure Projections

Developing accurate income and spending estimates is a critical component of operating a profit-oriented firm. These forecasts allow you to understand how much money you may anticipate making and how much it will cost to manage your firm. With precise estimates, you can make educated choices regarding pricing, marketing, and other parts of your organization that might affect profitability.

These are some strategies to take when establishing realistic income and spending projections:

1. **Collect historical data:** Look at your prior financial records and sales data to understand your business's trends and tendencies. This data may give insights into your income sources, costs, and places where you might enhance profitability.

2. **Assess the market:** Do market research to determine the demand for your product or service and how your rivals are pricing their offers. This information might allow you to create realistic revenue objectives and analyze your prospective consumer base.

3. **Estimate revenue:** Based on your previous data and market research, estimate how much revenue you may anticipate producing each month or quarter. Analyze elements such as seasonality, marketing initiatives, and changes in the market that may affect sales.

4. **Project Costs:** Estimate your fixed and variable expenses, such as rent, wages, supplies, and marketing costs. Make careful to evaluate any additional expenditures you may incur as your firm expands.

5. **Monitor your forecasts:** Periodically examine your estimates and compare them to your actual income and costs. This can allow you to find areas where you need to modify your strategy or costs to boost profitability.

6. **Modify as needed:** As you acquire more data and understand the market better, alter your revenue and spending predictions appropriately. Regularly reviewing and

revising your predictions can allow you to remain on track and accomplish your profit-oriented objectives.

In conclusion, developing realistic income and spending predictions is a vital step in operating a profit-oriented firm. By obtaining historical data, assessing the market, predicting income and forecasting costs, monitoring estimates, and changing as required, you can remain on pace to reach your profitability targets. Remember to remain adaptable and change your predictions as your firm develops to guarantee continuing success.

Utilizing Financial Planning to Increase Profitability

Financial planning is a key instrument for enhancing profitability in a profit-oriented firm. It entails constructing a thorough strategy to manage the company's finances, including budgeting, forecasting, and defining financial objectives. By adopting financial planning to boost profitability, organizations may better understand their financial status, make educated choices, and accomplish their financial goals.

Following are some ways that financial planning may be utilized to boost profitability in a profit-oriented business:

1. **Budgeting:** Budgeting is a vital component of financial planning, and it

entails making a strategy for how the organization will spend its money over a given time. By setting a budget, firms may manage expenditures, minimize overspending, and allocate resources to optimize revenue.

2. Forecasting: Forecasting includes projecting future financial results based on previous data and market patterns. Through forecasting, firms may predict changes in the market, prepare for future risks and opportunities, and make educated choices to increase profitability.

3. Establishing financial objectives: Financial planning entails creating specified, measurable, attainable, relevant, and time-bound (SMART) financial goals for the organization. These objectives might include generating revenue, lowering expenditures, improving profit margins, or attaining a specified degree of profitability. By creating clear financial objectives, firms may concentrate their efforts and resources on attaining them and monitor their progress toward profitability.

4. Cost management: Financial planning may help firms discover areas where they can decrease costs without sacrificing quality or efficiency. By examining expenditures and identifying methods to cut them, firms may boost profitability without compromising performance.

5. Cash flow management: Cash flow management is another crucial part of financial planning that includes monitoring the entry and outflow of cash in the firm. By managing cash flow properly, companies may guarantee that they have enough cash on hand to meet expenditures, invest in growth prospects, and achieve profitability.

In conclusion, financial planning is a significant instrument for boosting profitability in a profit-oriented firm.

Through budgeting, forecasting, defining financial objectives, controlling expenses, and monitoring cash flow, companies may improve their financial situation, make educated choices, and achieve long-term profitability.

PART II

Maximize Revenue

Maximize Revenue

Maximizing revenue is one of the major aims of a profit-oriented firm. Revenue is the entire amount of money a firm obtains from selling its goods or services. By growing sales, a corporation may raise its profitability and produce returns for its shareholders.

Following are some ways for boosting revenue in a profit-oriented business:

1. **Price plan:** One of the most effective methods to optimize revenue is a smart pricing strategy. A firm should consider elements such as market demand, competition, and expenses when determining to price of its goods or services. The aim is to establish the ideal pricing point that will maximize income while yet being competitive in the market.

2. **Product or service mix:** A firm should consider providing a variety of goods or

services to optimize income. This includes examining which items or services are the most lucrative and working on marketing or increasing those offers. The firm can also explore introducing complimentary items or services that might enhance total income.

3. **Upselling and cross-selling:** Another technique to optimize income is by upselling and cross-selling. This entails enticing consumers to acquire extra items or services or to upgrade to a more costly choice. This may be done via efficient sales strategies or by giving discounts for combining items or services.

4. **Marketing and advertising:** Good marketing and advertising may boost brand recognition, bring visitors to the firm, and eventually increase income. A firm should consider investing in targeted advertising, social media marketing, and other promotional strategies to reach its target demographic.

5. **Client retention:** A loyal customer base is vital for optimizing income. A firm should work on maintaining current customers by providing good customer service, giving loyalty awards, and creating a pleasant customer experience.

In conclusion, boosting revenue is a vital component of a profit-oriented firm. By executing a price plan, optimizing the product or service mix, applying upselling and cross-selling strategies, investing in marketing and advertising, and concentrating on client retention, a firm may raise its revenue and profitability.

Chapter 4

Pricing Strategies

Price is a vital part of every business's profitability and success. A profit-oriented pricing strategy includes establishing prices to maximize profits while taking into consideration consumer demand and competition in the market.

These are some pricing techniques that organizations might employ to become more profit-oriented:

1. Cost-plus pricing: Cost-plus pricing includes adding a markup to the product's cost to calculate its selling price. This pricing plan guarantees that the firm pays its expenses and earns a profit margin.

2. Value-based pricing: Value-based pricing entails determining prices based on the value that buyers perceive in the product. Companies may utilize customer surveys and market research to evaluate the value people put on the product and modify their pricing appropriately.

3. Price skimming: Price skimming includes establishing high pricing for new and innovative items when they are initially offered to the market. This method enables the firm to leverage early adopters' willingness to pay a premium price for the product.

4. Penetration pricing: Penetration pricing includes establishing cheap prices to acquire market share and draw consumers away from rivals. This approach may be beneficial in the long run if the firm can sustain its cheap pricing and acquire a large part of the market.

5. Psychosocial pricing: Psychological pricing includes establishing prices that appeal to buyers' emotions and perceptions. For example, placing pricing at $9.99 instead of $10.00 might make the product appear more reasonable to buyers.

6. Dynamic pricing: Dynamic pricing includes establishing prices that fluctuate depending on market demand and other criteria such as time of day, season, or location. This method enables firms to alter pricing in real-time to optimize profits.

7. Bundling: Bundling includes offering various items or services as a bundle for a cheaper price than if buyers were to purchase them separately. This method may enhance sales and profitability by enticing clients to purchase more than they first planned.

In conclusion, a profit-oriented pricing strategy entails establishing prices that maximize profits while taking into consideration consumer demand and competition in the market. Companies may employ numerous pricing techniques to become more profit-oriented, including cost-plus pricing, value-based pricing, price skimming, penetration pricing, psychological pricing, dynamic pricing, and bundling. By knowing the different pricing methods and their possible advantages, organizations may build a pricing plan that is personalized to their unique requirements and objectives.

The Significance of Pricing in Profitability

Price is a critical aspect of profitability for any profit-oriented firm. The price a firm sets for its goods or services significantly affects its revenue and profit margins. Establishing the proper pricing is vital to ensuring that a firm can pay its expenses, create profits, and stay competitive in the market.

Following are some reasons why the price is vital for the success for a profit-oriented business:

1. **Revenue Generation:** Price is closely tied to revenue generation. A firm has to establish a price that covers its expenses and produces enough income to earn a profit. A firm that sets pricing too low may not earn enough money, whereas a business that sets prices too high may dissuade consumers from making a purchase.

2. **Profit Margins:** Profit margins are the difference between the revenue earned and the expenses paid to provide the product or service. A firm that sets the correct pricing may guarantee that its profit margins are healthy and sustainable over the long run. Profit margins are crucial to the success of any profit-oriented firm since they enable the business to reinvest in development and prospects.

3. **Competition:** Price also plays a crucial part in defining a business's competitiveness in the market. A firm that delivers a product or service at a cheaper price than its rivals might attract more consumers, increase its market share, and produce larger profits. Yet, putting prices too low may also diminish the perceived value of the product or service, which can severely affect profitability.

4. **Consumer Perception:** Price may also impact the impression of the business's product or service. Consumers may connect a greater price with better quality or value. Hence, establishing a higher price may attract clients who are ready to pay more for perceived quality. Nonetheless, it is crucial to ensure that the pricing is not set excessively high, since this will dissuade clients from making a purchase.

5. **Flexibility:** Price also allows firms freedom to adapt their pricing approach

depending on market demand, changes in expenses, or other external variables. A firm that can modify its pricing fast and efficiently may capitalize on market possibilities and retain profitability over the long run.

In conclusion, price is a critical aspect of success for every profit-oriented organization. A firm has to establish the correct pricing to guarantee that it earns enough revenue to pay its expenses and create a profit. A well-designed price plan may also help a firm stay competitive in the market, attract consumers, and maintain good profit margins over the long run.

How to Develop Effective Pricing Strategies

Establishing an efficient pricing plan is vital for every profit-oriented firm. A well-planned pricing strategy may allow a corporation to optimize earnings, attract and keep consumers, and achieve a competitive edge.

Here are some measures to build a successful pricing strategy:

1. **Understanding your expenses:** When determining the price, it is necessary to understand the costs involved in manufacturing and distributing your goods or services. This comprises the cost of supplies, labor, overhead, and any additional charges. Understanding your expenditures can help you establish the least amount you need to charge to cover your expenses and earn a profit.

2. **Establish your price objectives:** After you know your expenses, you need to define your price targets. Are you attempting to maximize earnings, expand market share, or

maintain a specific level of revenue? Your pricing goals will drive your pricing choices and help you find the optimal price for your goods or services.

3. **Research your market:** It is crucial to study your market to understand your client's requirements, tastes, and willingness to spend. Evaluate your rivals' pricing methods, strengths, and shortcomings, and identify where you may position yourself in the market. This can help you choose the proper pricing for your goods or services and distinguish yourself from the competition.

4. **Consider your value proposition:** Your value proposition is what sets you different from your competition and what your consumers appreciate about your goods or services. Assess the value you are delivering to your clients and charge appropriately. If you are delivering a premium product or service, you may charge premium pricing.

5. **Test and adapt:** After you have chosen your pricing plan, it is crucial to test it and change it as required. Track your sales and profit margins, obtain client feedback, and alter your pricing plan appropriately. Constantly tweaking your pricing approach can help you optimize earnings and keep a competitive advantage.

In conclusion, having an effective pricing plan is crucial for every profit-oriented organization. By understanding your expenses, setting your price targets, studying your market, evaluating your value offer, and testing and changing your plan, you can design a pricing strategy that optimizes profits and keeps you competitive in your market.

Chapter 5

Sales and Marketing Techniques

Sales and marketing methods are vital for any organization trying to expand and prosper. These approaches encompass numerous strategies and procedures aimed at recruiting new clients, keeping current ones, and eventually generating income.

Following are some regularly used sales and marketing tactics:

• **Advertisement:** Advertising is a basic marketing approach that comprises paid advertising across different media channels, such as TV, radio, print, internet, and social media. Advertising is intended at building brand recognition, stimulating interest in the product or service, and driving sales.

•**Sales promotions:** Sales promotions are temporary incentives or discounts that are presented to consumers to entice them to make a purchase. Examples of sales promotions include coupons, free samples, sweepstakes, and loyalty programs.

• **Public relations:** Public relations entails managing a company's reputation and creating connections with stakeholders such as consumers, workers, investors, and the media. Public relations strategies include media relations, event planning, crisis management, and social responsibility programs.

• **Content marketing:** Content marketing entails generating and distributing useful and relevant information to attract and maintain a target audience. Content may comprise blog articles, videos, infographics, e-books, and social media postings. The purpose of content marketing is to position the organization as an expert in its sector, develop brand recognition, and eventually drive sales.

- **Search engine optimization (SEO):** SEO is a digital marketing approach that includes enhancing a website's content and structure to rank higher on search engine results pages. The purpose of SEO is to enhance organic traffic to the website and eventually produce more leads and sales.

- **Influencer marketing:** Influencer marketing entails teaming with social media influencers or celebrities to promote a product or service. Influencer marketing may be a very successful approach for reaching a new audience and building brand recognition.

- **Personal selling:** Personal selling is a one-on-one conversation between a salesman and a prospective customer. This strategy may be incredibly successful in creating connections, resolving consumer complaints, and closing purchases.

In conclusion, sales and marketing methods are vital for the success of any firm. By adopting a mix of these strategies, companies may attract new consumers, retain current ones, improve brand recognition, and eventually generate revenue. It's crucial for firms to examine which approaches are most successful for their target audience and sector, and to consistently adapt and enhance their strategy.

Leveraging Marketing to Drive Revenue Growth

For profit-oriented firms, revenue growth is crucial to establishing success and maintaining profitability over the long term. Marketing may be a strong instrument to assist generate revenue development by acquiring new clients, maintaining current ones, and boosting sales volume.

Here are some significant tactics that firms may utilize to use marketing to promote revenue growth:

A. **Create a thorough marketing plan:** To drive revenue development, organizations must have a clear and well-defined marketing strategy that includes their target audience, value proposition, marketing channels, and key performance indicators (KPIs) (KPIs). The strategy should be connected with the company's overarching goals and objectives and be continuously evaluated and revised as appropriate.

B. **Concentrate on client acquisition:** Gaining new customers is a vital component of revenue development. To attract new consumers, firms should spend on focused advertising campaigns, social media marketing, content marketing, and search engine optimization (SEO) (SEO). They should also ensure that their website is optimized for lead generation and conversion.

C. **Maintain current consumers:** Keeping existing customers is equally as vital as getting new ones. Companies should concentrate on delivering great customer service, creating strong client connections, and giving loyalty programs or other incentives to promote repeat purchases.

D. **Upsell and cross-sell:** Upselling and cross-selling are excellent techniques to boost sales volume and revenue per client.

Companies should evaluate client data to uncover chances to provide complementary goods or services to their current consumer base.

E. Utilize data-driven marketing: Data-driven marketing entails leveraging customer data to guide marketing strategy and approaches. By researching consumer behavior, organizations may uncover trends, preferences, and chances for development. Companies may utilize this data to customize marketing campaigns, target certain client categories, and optimize their marketing spend for optimal Return.

F. Measure and optimize: To drive revenue growth via marketing, firms must consistently assess and optimize their marketing activities. They should frequently examine KPIs, analyze consumer data, and test and adjust marketing tactics to guarantee they are providing the expected outcomes.

In summary, marketing may be a potent driver of revenue development for profit-oriented firms. By building a complete marketing plan, concentrating on client acquisition and retention, upselling and cross-selling, employing data-driven marketing, and evaluating and improving their efforts, organizations may achieve sustainable revenue growth over the long term.

Sales Strategies to Boost Earnings

If you're operating a profit-oriented firm, growing sales is crucial to reaching your financial objectives. Here are some sales tactics you may utilize to enhance profits:

A. **Know your customers:** To improve sales, you need to know your clients and understand their demands. Do market research to find out what your clients are seeking and how you might address their demands. Utilize this information to adjust your sales presentation and marketing communications.

B. **Upselling and cross-selling:** After you have a consumer interested in buying from you, employ upselling and cross-selling strategies to improve the transaction value. Provide complimentary items or services that will improve the customer's experience or answer an issue they may have.

C. **Concentrate on benefits, not features:** When marketing your goods or services, emphasize the advantages they bring, not simply the features. Demonstrate to your consumers how your product or service will make their lives simpler, save them time or money, or enhance their quality of life.

D. **Provide discounts and promotions:** Providing discounts or promotions might motivate consumers to make a purchase they would not have otherwise done. Employ limited-time specials, package deals, or loyalty programs to incentivize people to purchase from you.

E. **Follow up with consumers:** Following up with customers after a transaction might enhance the possibility of them making another purchase in the future. Send customized thank-you letters, ask for feedback, or give unique offers to recurring customers.

F. **Enhance your sales process:** Evaluate your sales process to discover any bottlenecks or places that may be improved. Simplify the process, educate your sales force, and invest in sales technology to make the process more efficient.

G. **Develop connections:** Establishing ties with your consumers may lead to repeat business and favorable word-of-mouth recommendations. Follow up with consumers periodically, communicate with them on social media, and give outstanding customer service.

By applying these sales strategies, you may improve sales and earnings for your profit-oriented firm. Remember to concentrate on giving value to your clients and creating solid connections, since this will lead to long-term success.

PART III

Managing Expenses

Managing Expenses

Managing expenses is vital for every profit-oriented firm since it immediately impacts the bottom line. A firm that can successfully control its costs may boost its profitability and stay competitive in the market.

Following are some ways for reducing expenses in a profit-oriented business:

1. Identify and prioritize expenditures: The first stage in limiting costs is to identify and prioritize expenses. Companies should divide their costs into essential and non-essential areas. Essential expenditures are those that are required for the company to run, whereas non-essential expenses are those that may be lowered or eliminated without harming the fundamental activities of the firm. Prioritizing spending will assist the firm to concentrate on cutting costs where it counts most.

2. Employ cost-saving measures: After expenditures are prioritized, the firm may apply cost-saving initiatives. This may involve negotiating better pricing with suppliers, lowering energy use, outsourcing non-core services, or using technological solutions that simplify operations and decrease manual labor.

3. Constantly evaluate and alter budgets: A budget is a helpful tool for controlling expenses. Companies should routinely examine their budgets to verify that they are on pace to accomplish financial objectives. Changes may need to be made if costs are greater than planned or income is lower than predicted.

4. Invest in staff training and development: Workers play a crucial role in controlling expenses. By investing in training and development, firms may enhance employee skills and productivity, which can lead to cost savings in the long term. For example, staff who are taught good time management practices may minimize labor expenses by working more effectively.

5. Measure and evaluate performance: Companies should measure and analyze performance to discover areas where expenses may be lowered. Performance measures, such as inventory turnover, labor productivity, and overhead expenses, may give significant insights into where costs are being spent and where improvements can be made.

In conclusion, managing expenses is a vital component of operating a profit-oriented firm. By recognizing and prioritizing expenditures, adopting cost-saving measures, routinely evaluating budgets, investing in personnel training and development, and monitoring and assessing performance, organizations may efficiently control costs and boost profitability.

Chapter 6

Handling Costs

Controlling expenditures is a critical component of operating a profit-oriented firm. To earn profits, a firm must guarantee that its costs do not exceed its income.

These are some strategies for controlling expenditures in a profit-oriented business:

1. **Establish a budget:** A budget is a blueprint that directs the firm on how much money it may spend on certain costs. It is crucial to make a budget that is reasonable and feasible. The budget should cover all the required expenditures, such as rent, utilities,

wages, and marketing, as well as some contingency reserves for unforeseen needs.

2. **Monitor costs:** Keeping track of spending is vital to guarantee that the organization remains within its budget. By constantly monitoring costs, a firm may discover areas where it is overpaying and make modifications to bring the expenses back in line with the budget.

3. **Prioritize spending:** Not all expenses are created equal, and some expenses are more vital to the firm than others. For example, investing in staff training or modernizing equipment may have a favorable influence on production and profitability. On the other side, overpaying for non-essential costs might affect the bottom line. It is necessary to prioritize costs and concentrate on those that have the most significant influence on the business's performance.

4. **Negotiate with suppliers:** It is always worth bargaining with vendors to achieve the best possible rates for products and services. By bargaining with suppliers, a firm may cut its expenditures and improve its revenues.

5. **Employ technology:** Technology may be a fantastic tool for controlling spending. There are several software solutions available that may help organizations manage costs, set budgets, and evaluate spending trends. By leveraging technology, a firm may acquire insights into its spending and discover areas where it can minimize costs.

6. **Check to spend periodically:** It is crucial to constantly analyze expenses to ensure that the firm is remaining on track with its budget. By analyzing costs periodically, a firm may discover patterns and alter its spending as required.

In conclusion, controlling expenditures is vital for a profit-oriented organization. By defining a budget, managing spending, prioritizing expenses, negotiating with suppliers, employing technology, and evaluating expenses periodically, a firm may guarantee that its expenses do not exceed its income and that it can produce profits in the long run.

Understanding Various Forms of Costs

As a profit-oriented company owner, it is vital to understand the many sorts of costs that your organization incurs. By classifying expenditures and understanding their influence on your bottom line, you can make educated choices regarding cost management, planning, and pricing.

These are some of the numerous sorts of expenditures that your firm may incur:

- **Fixed expenditures:** These are expenses that do not alter with changes in your company activity or sales volume. Examples of fixed expenditures include rent, salary, insurance payments, and property taxes. Fixed costs are important to keep your company functioning and are often incurred on a monthly or annual basis.

- **Variable expenditures:** These are costs that fluctuate with variations in your company activity or sales volume. Examples of variable expenditures include raw materials, manufacturing costs, and sales commissions. Variable expenditures may be handled by managing the volume of sales or the cost of items sold.

- **Direct expenditures:** These are costs that are directly tied to the production of a product or service. Examples of direct expenditures include supplies, labor, and shipping charges. Direct expenditures may be reduced by controlling the manufacturing process, negotiating rates with suppliers, and increasing efficiency.

- **Indirect expenditures:** These are expenses that are not directly connected to the manufacturing of a product or service but are required for operating the company. Examples of indirect expenditures include rent, utilities, and office supplies. Indirect expenditures may be managed by minimizing wasteful spending and obtaining better prices with suppliers.

- **Periodic costs:** These are expenses that occur sporadically or periodically. Examples of recurrent expenditures include yearly taxes, equipment upkeep, and legal bills. Periodic costs may be prepared for by putting aside monies in advance or by budgeting for them regularly.

- **Capital costs:** These are expenses that are spent to purchase or enhance long-term assets, such as equipment, buildings, or land. Capital costs are often depreciated over time and may have a substantial influence on your business's profitability. Capital costs may be minimized by prioritizing investments and funding them effectively.

In conclusion, recognizing the many kinds of expenditures that your firm incurs is crucial for making educated choices regarding cost management, planning, and pricing. By controlling expenditures correctly, you may increase your business's profitability and assure its long-term success.

Cost-Reducing Techniques for Increasing Profitability

For a profit-oriented firm, boosting profitability is vital for long-term viability and development. One method to do this is by employing cost-cutting techniques. These are some cost-cutting techniques that firms might pursue to boost profitability:

• **Do a cost study:** Companies should undertake a comprehensive review of all their expenditures to discover areas where costs may be lowered. This might involve reviewing electricity bills, office supplies, equipment upkeep, and other overhead expenditures.

• **Adopt energy-efficient measures:** Applying energy-efficient measures such as employing LED lighting, energy-efficient equipment, and programmable thermostats may considerably lower energy bills and save expenditures in the long run.

• **Negotiate with suppliers:** Companies may bargain with their suppliers for better pricing and discounts on large orders. It is also vital to examine supplier contracts often to ensure that the price stays competitive.

- **Minimize staff turnover:** Excessive employee turnover may be expensive for firms. It is necessary to establish a happy work atmosphere, offers competitive wages and benefits, and engage in employee training and development to lower turnover rates.

- **Outsource non-core operations:** Outsourcing non-core functions such as accounting, IT services, and human resources may reduce expenses and enable firms to concentrate on their core activities and produce income.

- **Deploy technology solutions:** Adopting technology solutions like automation, cloud computing, and collaboration tools may enhance efficiency, cut expenses, and boost productivity.

- **Reduce needless spending:** Companies should analyze all expenses frequently to discover excessive costs that may be eliminated. This might involve decreasing non-essential travel, lowering workplace space, and cutting down on needless subscriptions or memberships.

In summary, applying cost-cutting methods may help firms enhance profitability and achieve long-term sustainability. It is crucial to do a complete review of all expenditures, negotiate with suppliers, decrease staff turnover, outsource non-core tasks, apply technological solutions, and eliminate superfluous expenses to achieve cost reductions. By adopting a deliberate approach to cost-cutting, firms may lower expenditures while retaining their capacity to create revenue and thrive.

Chapter 7

Inventory and Supply Chain Management

Inventory and supply chain management are key components of every profit-oriented firm. Proper management of inventory and supply chain may help organizations decrease costs, boost efficiency, and improve customer satisfaction, eventually leading to higher profitability.

¤ Inventory Management:

Good inventory management requires balancing the expense of inventory with the requirement to satisfy consumer demand. Excess inventory locks up cash and raises the danger of products becoming outmoded or damaged, while inadequate inventory may lead to stockouts and missed revenues.

A profit-oriented firm has to employ tactics such as just-in-time inventory management, demand forecasting, and inventory optimization to maintain a healthy inventory level. Utilizing inventory management software may help organizations maintain inventory levels, streamline order processing, and decrease mistakes.

¤ Supply Chain Management:

A supply chain covers all the operations involved in the transportation of products and services from suppliers to consumers. Controlling the supply chain properly may save costs, improve delivery times, and raise customer happiness.

A profit-oriented firm should work on improving the supply chain to decrease costs and enhance efficiency. This might involve creating strong connections with suppliers, applying lean manufacturing practices, and enhancing logistics management.

Utilizing technology such as supply chain management software may also help organizations monitor supplier performance, simplify order processing, and increase engagement with suppliers and customers.

Advantages of Good Inventory and Supply Chain Management:

Good inventory and supply chain management may have considerable advantages for a profit-oriented organization, including:

• **Reduce expenses:** By managing inventory and supply chain, firms may decrease costs related to inventory carrying, transportation, and logistics.

- **Improved efficiency:** Efficient inventory and supply chain management may enhance production efficiency, decrease lead times, and improve delivery times, eventually leading to greater customer satisfaction.

- **Increased customer happiness:** By ensuring items are in stock and delivered on schedule, companies may boost customer satisfaction and develop customer loyalty.

- **Better forecasting:** Good inventory and supply chain management may help organizations improve demand forecasts and decrease the risk of stockouts or overstocking.

In conclusion, inventory and supply chain management are key components of every profit-oriented firm. Good management may help firms cut expenses, enhance efficiency, and improve customer happiness, eventually leading to higher profitability. By implementing efficient tactics and employing technology, firms may improve their inventory and supply chain and achieve a competitive edge in the market.

The Importance of Inventory and Supply Chain Management in Profitability

Inventory and supply chain management play a vital role in the success of profit-oriented enterprises. Good inventory management ensures that a firm has the correct quantity of stock on hand to fulfill consumer demand while avoiding the expenses associated with excess inventory or stockouts. This, in turn, optimizes the potential for sales and revenue, which eventually influences profitability.

These are some ways that inventory and supply chain management affect profitability:

1. **Cost of goods sold (COGS):** Inventory management directly influences COGS, which is the cost of creating or obtaining the things that a corporation sells. By optimizing inventory levels, a corporation may maximize COGS by decreasing waste and limiting the expenses associated with excess inventory.

2. **Customer satisfaction:** Supply chain management plays a critical part in ensuring that a corporation can fulfill consumer demand. A well-managed supply chain ensures that items are delivered on time and in the proper amounts, which helps to generate customer loyalty and satisfaction. This, in turn, may lead to repeat business and greater sales.

3. **Cash flow:** Good inventory management may enhance cash flow by lowering the amount of capital locked up in surplus inventory. This allows a corporation to spend on other aspects of the business, such as marketing, research, and development, or

expansion, which may assist to generate growth and profitability.

4. **Risk management:** Controlling inventory levels and supply chain risks may assist to limit the possibility of stockouts or interruptions to the supply chain. This may avoid missed sales and income owing to unfilled orders or delays in delivery, which can significantly influence profitability.

5. **Efficiency:** An effective supply chain may lower the time and costs involved with delivering items to clients. This may boost profitability by decreasing expenses connected with logistics, storage, and transportation, which can be passed on to consumers or reinvested in the firm.

In conclusion, inventory and supply chain management are key components of a profit-oriented business's success. Effective management may reduce COGS, enhance customer happiness, boost cash flow, limit risk, and improve efficiency, all of which can significantly benefit profitability. By prioritizing inventory and supply chain management, organizations may guarantee that they are well-positioned for long-term profitability and success.

How to Improve Your Inventory and Supply Chain

Managing your inventory and supply chain may be a crucial aspect in enhancing profitability for your firm. By optimizing your inventory levels, limiting stockouts, and cutting supply chain expenses, you may enhance cash flow and boost earnings.

Here are some recommendations on how to improve your inventory and supply chain for a profit-oriented business:

1. **Employ forecasting and demand planning:** One of the most critical stages in managing your inventory and supply chain is to utilize forecasting and demand planning. By examining previous sales data, market trends, and other variables, you can precisely estimate future demand and manage your inventory levels appropriately. This may help you prevent overstocking or understocking, which can lead to increased inventory expenses or missed revenue.

2. **Adopt just-in-time (JIT) inventory management:** JIT inventory management is a method that includes receiving inventory only when it is required for production or sale. By lowering the quantity of inventory you retain, you may decrease carrying costs and free up cash flow. This technique needs close cooperation with suppliers to guarantee the timely delivery of items.

3. **Optimize your supply chain:** Streamlining your supply chain may cut costs

and enhance efficiency. Consider combining shipments, negotiating better terms with suppliers, and leveraging technology such as automated ordering systems to lessen the administrative effort.

4. **Track inventory turnover and days sales outstanding (DSO):** These indicators will help you assess how rapidly you are turning over goods and receiving payments from clients. By increasing these KPIs, you may minimize cash locked up in inventories and accounts receivable.

5. **Invest in technology:** Investing in technology such as inventory management systems and supply chain analytics may help you better manage your inventory and supply chain. These solutions may give real-time data on inventory levels, lead times, and other crucial parameters, enabling you to make better-educated choices.

In essence, improving your inventory and supply chain is crucial for a profit-oriented organization. By employing forecasting and demand planning, adopting JIT inventory management, streamlining your supply chain, monitoring key indicators, and investing in technology, you may improve cash flow, cut costs, and boost profitability.

PART IV

Increasing Profitability Through Innovation

Increasing Profitability Through Innovation

Innovation is a vital driver of success for every profit-oriented firm. It may enable a firm to create new goods and services, enhance current ones, cut costs, and boost efficiency. By inventing, a firm may distinguish itself from rivals, grow its market share, and eventually create more revenue and profit.

These are some ways that a firm might boost profitability via innovation:

• **Create new goods and services:** By launching new products and services, a corporation may tap into new markets and improve income sources. Innovation may assist to find unmet client demands and produce new goods that fulfill those needs, therefore generating a competitive edge.

- **Streamline procedures and decrease costs:** Innovation may assist to discover inefficiencies in corporate processes and create innovative solutions to simplify operations. By cutting expenses and enhancing efficiency, a corporation may enhance its profit margins.

- **Adopt new technology:** Emerging technologies may allow a firm to automate operations, cut labor costs, and increase product quality. By adopting technology, a firm may remain ahead of the competition and boost profitability.

- **Enhance customer experience:** By leveraging innovation to improve the customer experience, a firm may boost customer happiness and loyalty, leading to higher sales and profit. This may be done via new technology, enhanced service offerings, or other innovations that improve the customer experience.

- **Collaborate with others:** Cooperation with other enterprises, academic institutions, or research groups may lead to fresh insights and ideas that can enable a company to innovate. Cooperation may also assist to share expenses and lessen risks involved with innovation.

In conclusion, innovation is a critical component of boosting profitability for a profit-oriented firm. By producing new goods and services, optimizing operations, embracing new technology, enhancing customer experience, and partnering with others, a firm may distinguish itself from rivals, raise sales, and eventually produce more profit. By making innovation a priority, a firm may develop a sustainable competitive edge and position itself for long-term success.

Chapter 8

Innovation and Growth

Innovation is a vital engine of development for profit-oriented enterprises. It lets firms create new goods, services, and processes that may boost revenue and profitability. Companies that embrace innovation and implement it into their plans are more likely to flourish and survive in today's continuously changing business climate.

These are some ways that innovation might generate growth for profit-oriented businesses:

• **New goods and services:** Innovation may help firms to produce new products and services that fit the shifting demands of consumers. This may establish new income sources and boost profitability.

- **Enhanced processes:** Innovation may also lead to improvements in processes, such as manufacturing, supply chain, and distribution. This may boost efficiency, cut expenses, and improve profitability.

- **Competitive advantage:** Businesses that can innovate and produce distinctive goods, services, and processes may obtain a competitive edge in the market. This might allow them to acquire new clients and improve market share.

- **New markets:** Innovation may also enable firms to grow into new markets. By designing goods or services that are suited to the demands of new clients or markets, firms may tap into new sources of income and growth.

- **Brand building:** Innovation may also enable firms to establish their brand and reputation. By providing unique goods and services, companies may position themselves as leaders in their sector and cultivate a devoted consumer base.

To stimulate innovation and drive development, profit-oriented firms should build a culture that appreciates and fosters creativity. This might entail investing in research and development, giving resources and support for innovation, and rewarding people for creative ideas and efforts.

In conclusion, innovation is crucial for development and profitability in today's corporate climate. Profit-oriented firms that welcome innovation and implement it into their strategy are more likely to flourish and survive in the long run. By producing new goods and services, improving processes, obtaining a competitive edge, tapping into new markets, and strengthening their brand, organizations may achieve growth and profitability via innovation.

The Importance of Innovation in Business Profitability

Innovation has a key role in increasing company success for profit-oriented firms. Innovation entails producing new goods, processes, or business models that fulfill growing consumer wants and offer new market possibilities. By developing new goods and services, firms may acquire a competitive edge, improve their market share, and raise their profitability.

These are some of the primary ways in which innovation may drive corporate profitability:

1. Improved revenue: Innovative goods and services may attract new clients and allow firms to extend their market share. By satisfying client demands that are not being satisfied by current goods or services, firms may gain a bigger portion of the market and create higher income.

2. Greater margins: New goods and services might fetch higher pricing than established items, which can lead to better profit margins. This is particularly true if the invention is protected by patents or other intellectual property rights, which might restrict rivals from duplicating the idea and competing on price.

3. Cost savings: Innovation may also enable organizations to decrease their expenses by adopting more efficient processes or employing new materials that are less costly. This may lead to higher profitability by decreasing the cost of manufacturing products or providing services.

4. Brand differentiation: By providing new goods and services, companies may distinguish their brand from rivals and develop a distinct selling proposition. This may assist them to charge higher pricing and build client loyalty, which can lead to greater profitability over the long run.

5. Improved productivity: Innovation may also promote productivity improvements by providing new technology or procedures that simplify operations and decrease waste. This may lead to better efficiency and decreased expenses, which can promote profitability.

In conclusion, innovation plays a significant role in boosting company success for profit-oriented firms. By providing new goods and services, firms may boost revenue, enhance profit margins, decrease expenses, distinguish their brand, and increase productivity. To attain these advantages, firms must emphasize innovation and engage in research and development to produce goods and services that suit shifting consumer wants and generate new market possibilities.

How to Create a Culture of Creativity

In today's fast-changing business climate, promoting a culture of innovation is crucial for every profit-oriented corporation. Innovation may allow a firm to remain competitive, develop, and fulfill the growing demands of its consumers.

These are some strategies to build a culture of innovation:

- **Promote Risk-Taking:** Creativity typically includes taking chances, therefore it's crucial to build a culture where people feel empowered to take risks and attempt new things. Leaders should promote innovation, and reward people who take measured risks.

- **Create a Diverse Team:** A varied team brings unique viewpoints and experiences to the table, which may lead to fresh and inventive ideas. Promote diversity in recruiting and seek out workers from diverse origins and with varied skill sets.

- **Promote Collaboration:** Creativity is typically the outcome of cooperation between people and teams. Establish a work climate that fosters cooperation and open communication, and gives tools and resources to assist collaboration.

- **Offer Resources for Innovation:** Give workers the resources and assistance they need to innovate. This might include access to training and development programs, financing for research and development, and access to cutting-edge technology.

- **Celebrate Success:** Celebrate and praise workers who come up with unique ideas or contribute to successful initiatives.

Acknowledging and rewarding unique thinking may assist to develop a culture of innovation and inspire others to submit their ideas.

- **Create a Learning Culture:** Promote continual learning and development by offering chances for workers to acquire new skills, attend conferences or seminars, and take on new tasks. A learning culture may help workers remain motivated and engaged, and can lead to new and inventive ideas.

In conclusion, promoting a culture of innovation is vital for every profit-oriented organization that wants to remain competitive and fulfill the growing requirements of its consumers. By promoting risk-taking, developing a diverse workforce, encouraging collaboration, giving resources for innovation, rewarding achievement, and cultivating a learning culture, firms may create an atmosphere where innovation flourishes.

Chapter 9

Diversification and Expansion

Diversification and growth are two tactics that profit-oriented firms may employ to enhance revenue, profitability, and market share. These methods entail taking measured risks and investing resources in new markets, goods, or services to generate growth and improve profitability.

Diversification entails increasing a business's product range or entering new markets to decrease risk and improve income streams. For example, a garment firm may diversify by introducing a line of accessories or expanding into overseas markets. By diversifying, the firm may lessen its dependency on a particular product or market, and generate new prospects for development and profitability.

The expansion entails growing a business's capacity or presence in its current markets. This may be done by adding additional sites, increasing product lines, or purchasing other firms. For example, a restaurant chain may grow by adding additional sites in other cities or by purchasing a competitor restaurant chain. By growing, the firm may improve its market share and reach a larger audience, resulting in higher revenue and profits.

Both diversification and growth need careful planning, research, and expenditure. Companies must carefully examine the possible risks and benefits of any strategy and ensure they have the resources and competence to execute the plan effectively.

The following are some advantages of diversity and expansion:

A. **Increased revenue:** Diversification and growth may enhance a business's revenue by introducing new sources of income or by increasing current revenue streams.

B. **Reduced risk:** Diversification may decrease risk by spreading out a business's investments over several goods or markets, which can assist to lessen the effect of economic downturns or changes in customer behavior.

C. **Increased market share:** Growth may assist a firm to get a bigger portion of its current market, which can lead to higher revenue and profitability.

D. **Improved competitiveness:** Diversification and growth may enable a firm to remain competitive by providing new goods or services and by reaching new consumers.

In conclusion, diversification and growth are successful strategies for profit-oriented organizations to enhance revenue, profitability, and market share. Yet, these methods take careful preparation and investment, and firms must ensure they have the resources and experience to implement the strategy effectively.

Tips for Growing Your Business

Growing a firm is a crucial step toward growth and success. Yet, it takes careful planning and execution to guarantee that the growth is profitable. Here are some ways for developing your company with a profit-oriented approach:

- **Market Research:** Doing market research to understand the target audience and their demands is crucial before developing the firm. Evaluate the market demand for your product or service and assess whether there is a need for growth. Look at competition to uncover possibilities to stand out in the market.

•**Build a Business Plan:** Creating a complete business plan that covers the growth strategy, financial predictions, and possible hazards is crucial. The plan should define the aims and objectives of the expansion, the resources necessary, and the timescale for execution.

• **Diversify Your Goods or Services:** Diversification helps improve your consumer base and income sources. Offer new items or services that complement your present ones or expand into a new market niche. This might allow you to acquire a competitive advantage and reach new consumers.

• **Utilize Technology:** Technology may assist firms to simplify processes, decreasing expenses, and reaching a bigger audience.

Investment in technology may assist companies to automate operations, enhancing efficiency, and boosting production.

- **Increase Your Reach:** Try growing your company geographically by adding additional sites or increasing your online presence. This may assist to reach a bigger consumer base and improve income.

- **Establish Strategic Partnerships:** Connecting with other firms that complement your products may assist to grow your reach and improve income. Look for alliances that give mutual advantages and correspond with your company's aims.

- **Monitor Financial Metrics:** Maintain a tight check on important financial data like sales, profit margin, and cash flow. Constantly assess and alter your company strategy depending on these data to guarantee that the growth is profitable.

In conclusion, extending your firm may be an excellent method to boost profitability. Yet, it takes careful preparation, implementation, and continuous monitoring to assure success. Employ these tactics to build your firm while retaining a profit-oriented mindset.

How to Diversify Your Revenue Sources

Diversifying your income sources is a vital approach to maintaining the long-term prosperity of your firm. By having several sources of income, you may lessen your dependency on any one specific source, and better weather economic downturns or changes in the market. Here are some strategies for diversifying your money streams:

1. Identify new goods or services: Look for chances to provide new products or services that complement your present offers. For example, if you own a restaurant, you may try providing catering services or selling branded items.

2. Expand into new markets: Try growing your firm into new geographic regions, either by establishing additional locations or by offering your goods or services online. This may help you reach a bigger audience and tap into new sources of money.

3. Create new income models: Look for methods to monetize your current assets in new ways. For example, if you have a significant social media following, you may explore delivering sponsored content or advertising on your platform.

4. Utilize technology: Discover how technology may help you diversify your income sources. For example, if you operate a brick-and-mortar business, you may consider developing an e-commerce website or providing online ordering and delivery.

5. Collaborate with other firms: Look for possibilities to partner with other businesses in your sector or similar areas. For example, if you own a gym, you may collaborate with a health food shop to provide discounts or joint promotions.

6. Provide subscriptions or memberships: Consider selling subscriptions or memberships that give recurring income. For example, if you manage a beauty salon, you may provide a monthly membership service for frequent clients.

7. Monetize your data: Look for methods to monetize the data you acquire about your clients or operations. For example, if you manage a SaaS platform, you may explore providing analytics services or selling your data to third-party organizations.

In essence, diversifying your income sources is a vital approach to maintaining the long-term prosperity of your firm. By discovering new goods or services, expanding into new areas, generating new revenue models, utilizing technology, working with other companies, selling subscriptions or memberships, and monetizing your data, you may build a more robust and sustainable company model.

Conclusion

In conclusion, chasing profits is a crucial part of every company, as it allows firms to sustainably invest in growth, development, and innovation. It also offers a mechanism to reward investors, workers, and stakeholders for their efforts and dedication to the company's success. Nonetheless, it is vital to combine profitability with responsible and ethical procedures to guarantee the long-term survival and reputation of the organization. By emphasizing profitability with social and environmental responsibility, firms may generate value for their stakeholders while having a good influence on society and the planet at large.

PUTTING IT ALL TOGETHER

Being Profit Oriented

Being Profit Oriented

Being profit-oriented is a vital step for any company striving to achieve sustained development and success. A profit-oriented attitude demands a profound awareness of the aspects that lead to profitability, including revenue creation, cost management, and operational efficiency.

To become profit-oriented, firms must first identify their major income sources and prioritize operations that generate revenue development. This can entail investing in marketing and sales activities, developing new product lines, or expanding into new markets. Also, firms must work on controlling expenses by streamlining operational procedures, negotiating with suppliers, and discovering opportunities for cost reductions.

Another key part of being profit-oriented is developing a culture of responsibility and performance. This requires creating explicit objectives and targets, developing metrics to monitor progress, and holding staff responsible for reaching or surpassing these expectations. It also demands giving people the tools, resources, and training they need to thrive in their professions.

Lastly, firms must regularly evaluate and analyze their financial performance to discover opportunities for improvement and make strategic choices regarding investments, cost-cutting measures, and other efforts that might contribute to long-term success.

In essence, being profit-oriented demands a holistic strategy that involves revenue creation, cost management, operational efficiency, and a culture of responsibility and performance. By adopting a profit-oriented perspective, organizations may achieve sustainable development, provide value for their stakeholders, and position themselves for long-term success in a competitive economy.

Sustaining Profitability Over the Long-Term.

Sustaining profitability over the long term is vital for any firm that aims to attain sustained success. It demands a strategic strategy that combines short-term benefits with long-term development and profitability.

To retain profitability over the long term, firms must first have a comprehensive grasp of their financial condition, including revenue, costs, and cash flow. They must also examine their industry and competitive environment, identify trends and opportunities, and build a strategic plan that specifies their goals, objectives, and actions.

Once a strategic strategy is in place, organizations must concentrate on optimizing efficiency and production while reducing expenses and waste. This may entail investing in technology, simplifying procedures, and enhancing supply chain management.

Another essential component in retaining profitability over the long term is innovation. Companies must always innovate and adapt to changes in the market to stay competitive and fulfill changing client expectations. This may entail launching new goods or services, expanding into new markets, or embracing new technology.

Ultimately, organizations must prioritize their staff and consumers. By investing in staff training and development, establishing a happy work environment, and offering exceptional customer service, companies may generate a loyal customer base and a solid reputation, which can eventually lead to improved profitability over time.

In conclusion, sustaining profitability over the long term involves a diverse strategy that includes strategic planning, maximum efficiency, innovation, and a focus on staff and consumers. By implementing these ideas, firms may achieve sustained success and prosper in an ever-changing business climate.